Marty Nachel's
Beer Tasting Journal:
How to Evaluate and Enjoy
Your Favorite Beers

by Marty Nachel

About This Book

As someone who has dedicated more than half of my life to learning and teaching about quality beer and beer experiences, I think it's important to share what I've learned over the decades with others who share my love and passion for beer. That's why I want to guide others to focus not just on beer in general, but the nuances of style and the difference between good beer and not-so-good beer.

By keeping a journal or logbook of your beer drinking experiences, you'll become much more attuned to what differentiates one style from another, what differentiates one quality level from another, and–most importantly–what differentiates between those beers you enjoy and those beers you don't (and why).

How to Properly Taste Beer

To the vast majority of people who consume beer, tasting it is a simple pleasure–one that requires no cerebral effort to accomplish. To a select minority of people, however, tasting beer can be–and often is–a complex pleasure that demands that the brain be every bit as engaged as the palate.

There is, indeed, a proper way to taste beer if you identify with that select minority. Though there are no "rules" to enjoying beer, there are recommended practices to follow if you are evaluating and making comparisons between beers.

Always taste beer at the appropriate serving temperature.

Beer that is too cold can stunt your taste buds and your palate's ability to do what it's designed to do. Forty to forty-five degrees Fahrenheit (4.5 to 7 degrees Celsius) is the optimum sampling temperature across all beer styles.

Always decant the beer into a clean glass.

Beer was never meant to be consumed directly out of its container. Pouring beer into a glass accomplishes two things: it causes carbonation to break out of solution, which brings out more of the aromatics in the beer, and it also means you'll ingest less CO_2 as you drink the beer.

Try to evaluate the beer as objectively as possible.

It's okay to have an opinion about a beer, but that opinion should be based on something less subjective than your personal likes or dislikes. All beer-related observations should have a common and objective reference point, such as the beers' stylistic integrity.

About Beer Styles

There are over 100 different beer styles brewed around the world. Having a basic familiarity with how they are classified and differentiated is key to appreciating them fully.

So how are they classified and differentiated? Let's start with the two big "families" of beer styles: Ales and Lagers. Simply put, these two classes of beer are identified by how they are fermented.

Ales (the bigger "family") are fermented with what is referred to as top-fermenting yeast, and Lagers (the smaller "family") are fermented with what is referred to as bottom-fermenting yeast. In addition to this, ales are fermented at higher temperatures (think room temperature) and lagers are fermented at lower temperatures (typically between 40 and 50 degrees F.). Due to their warm temperatures, ales can finish fermenting in less time (3 - 4 weeks) than lagers, which can take up to twice as long to finish fermenting (6 - 8 weeks).

Due to the yeast type and warm fermentation, ales tend to be fruitier than lagers, whereas lagers tend to be much cleaner tasting due to the cold temperatures that stunt the production of fruitiness and other fermentation characteristics.

Most beer styles fall into these two classifications. Here are sample lists of ales and lagers, including their country of origin:

Ales

<u>Berliner Weisse</u> (Germany): A pale, tart and tangy wheat-based beer from Berlin, often infused with fruit flavoring to cut the acidity.

<u>Brown Ale</u> (UK): This style from the north of England is a chestnut-colored ale that is often described as having a caramel-toffee flavor with a light roasted note. It was considered the working man's beer for many years, but now seems to be in decline.

<u>Flanders Red</u> (Belgium): This reddish-brown fruity beer is among the most acidic beers in the world. It is aged in barrels, from which it gets its trademark woody character and sourness, and it is often referred to as the "Burgundy of Beer."

<u>Gose</u> (Germany): This pale and tart wheat-based beer is from the town of Goslar in northern Germany. In addition to traditional beer ingredients, Gose is also made with salt and coriander seed.

India Pale Ale/IPA (UK): This is a version of pale ale that was initially exported from England to ports in India. It features elevated bitterness and more intense overall hop character. In the U.S., regional versions are distinguishable between East Coast and West Coast.

Lambic (Belgium): This beer style is one of the very few beers left in the world that is "spontaneously fermented." Breweries in the Senne River Valley southwest of Brussels, rely on the microflora (wild yeast and friendly bacteria) in the region to kick start the fermentation of this pale, wheat-based beer. The result is a dry, fruity and sour beer that often requires some palate acclimation. When different vintages of Lambic are blended, they are then renamed "Gueuze."

New England IPA (US): This style took the market by storm in recent years. It is often referred to as being hazy or juicy, descriptors that both apply to these opaque and citrusy beers. The NEIPA designation is a misnomer, however, as these beers do not in any way resemble India Pale Ales.

Oud Bruin/Brune (Belgium): This beer features a unique malty-sour palate. Like its sister beer, Flanders red, it is also from the same region in Belgium, but unlike the Red, it is fermented and aged in stainless steel vats rather than barrels or foudres.

Pale ale (UK): Just as the name implies this beer is made from pale malts and is golden to amber in color. It often exhibits hoppy character (hop aroma, flavor and bitterness).

Porter (UK)- This dark brown beer traces its history back to London in the 1770s. It was at one time one of the most popular beers in Britain, but its popularity waned as Lagers became more prominent. Today there are two main types of Porter, the English Brown Porter and the darker, more hoppy American robust style. (see also Baltic Porter below)

Scotch Ale/Scottish Ale (UK)- Scotch Ales and Scottish Ales are essentially both made from the same ingredients, the main difference is in the amount of grain that is used to brew the beer. Scotch Ales are bigger bodied, bolder flavored and contain higher alcohol content. Scottish Ales are lighter bodied, milder flavored and contain lower alcohol content. All of these are brewed and sold according to their Shilling designation,a throwback to the days when beer was taxed based on its alcohol content. Scottish Ales are typically 40-, 50- and 60 Shilling, while Scotch Ales are typically 80 to 120 Shilling.

Stout (UK): The word stout was originally used as an adjective to describe a bolder and brawnier porter, but eventually became the style designation for the dark beer we now call Stout. And stout is not just a singular style, there are several sub-styles that include Dry Stout, Sweet Stout, Tropical Stout, Oatmeal Stout and Imperial Stout.

Trappist/Abbey Ales (Belgium): The religious order that is known as Trappist began brewing beer hundreds of years ago as a way to support the monastic lifestyle. Over time the Trappists introduced a variety of beer styles including Patersbier (table beer), Dubbel, Tripel and Quadrupel, all varying in color and alcohol intensity. "Trappist" is a protected appellation; breweries that are not owned or operated by a Trappist order cannot use the Trappist name on their beers. Secular breweries that produce Trappist-style beers must refer to their products as "Abbey," "Abbaye," "Abdij," or "Abt" beers.

Witbier/Biere Blanche (Belgium): Witbier means white beer in Flemish. This is a 400-year-old beer style from the town of Hoegaarden, Belgium. Pale and hazy appearance, it is citrusy due to its inclusion of coriander and orange peel.

Weissbier/weizenbier (Germany): This wheat-based s quencher is a Bavarian specialty. Weissbier means white beer, while Weizenbier means wheat beer, and both refer to the same style. Variations called hefeweizen simply note that the beer was bottled *"mit hefe."* (with yeast).

Lagers

Bock Beer (Germany): Bock beer is typified by the chestnut brown, malty, slightly higher in alcohol beer that many beer drinkers are familiar with. But Bock does have its sub-styles, which include Helles (pale) Bock, the hoppy Maibock (named for the month of May), the richly malted Doppelbock (double bock) and the enigmatic Eisbock (ice bock).

Dortmunder (Germany): This working-class favorite from Dortmund makes rare appearances outside the Fatherland. Crystal clear and golden, Dortmunder is not as hoppy as Pilsner and not as malty as most Bavarian favorites. Due to its high export numbers, it is often referred to as "Export Bier."

Marzenbier (Germany): Prior to the invention of artificial refrigeration, brewers in warmer climes took summers off and resumed brewing in the fall. Marzenbier was traditionally brewed in great quantities in the month of March (Marz) and was gradually consumed throughout the summer months.

Whatever was left in storage at harvest time was rolled out and riotously consumed at the autumn festivals; this later became known as Oktoberfest bier.

Munich Dunkel (Germany): Munich Dunkel (dark) is simply a darker and more flavorful version of the Munich Helles. It offers notes of nougat and chocolate, with a hint of roastiness.

Munich Helles (Germany): Bavarian brewers, due to their proximity to Alpine caves, quickly became experts at producing lager beers. The malty golden-amber Munich Helles (pale) became a staple throughout southern Germany.

Pilsner (Czech Republic): No other beer style in history has dominated the worldwide market like Pilsner has. Originally brewed at the Urquell Brewery in Plzen in 1842 in Bohemia, this golden lager was the first of its kind ever brewed. It went on to inspire countless brands, including many mass market beers, around the world since.

Rauchbier (Germany): This unique and somewhat esoteric beer from northern Bavaria (Franconia) is centered in the town of Bamberg. Its piquant smoky aroma and savory smoke flavor is a result of the brewers' use of malt that has been smoked over beechwood fires.

Schwarzbier (Germany): This black (schwarz) beer is somewhat of a rarity outside of Germany, which is kind of a shame. It is dark due to the use of roasted malts, but it is every bit as drinkable as any other German lager. In fact, many people refer to Schwarzbier as the black Pilsner.

Vienna Lager (Austria): In the late 1800's when German brewers seemed to be dominating the lager beer market, Austrian brewers were envious of their success. A convention of prominent Austrian brewers in Vienna decided to create their own style of beer intended to rival German Oktoberfest Bier. The result is the slightly darker and more complex Vienna lager beer.

Hybrids

Lastly, there is a third, very small category of beer styles that are considered *Hybrids* because they are created using a cross combination of yeast type and fermentation method. These include:

Altbier (Germany): Many cities throughout Germany (and Europe, for that matter) can claim their own specific beer style. Dusseldorf is one of those cities. The amber-tinged Altbier (old beer) is relatively rare outside of Dusseldorf; it is both richly malted and firmly bittered, one of the few beer styles that can claim to be so.

Baltic porter (Estonia, Latvia, Lithuania): Porter was a very popular beer in Britain as well as many other countries to which the style was exported. At higher latitudes in the Baltic states, brewers took to brewing this beer to a higher gravity, as well as fermenting this traditional ale at lower temperature. The resulting beer is a very dark and strong version of porter.

Poland is currently one of the largest producers of Baltic Porter.

California Common (USA): This fruity, toasty, amber colored beer is strongly associated with the state of California. During the Gold Rush, when thousands of people headed West to strike their claim, many breweries sprung up to slake their thirsts. But artificial refrigeration was hardly known at the time, so even though lager yeast was being used, the fermentations were quite warm. This led to the fermentation vessels hissing or "steaming," which gave rise to the now trademarked name, Steam Beer™.

Cream ale (USA): This crisp, pale beer is uniquely American. Though it looks like a pilsner, its "corny" aroma usually lets you know it's a Cream Ale. This beer is fermented with ale yeast but at cold temperatures.

Kolsch (Germany): In the city of Koln (Cologne in the French tongue), a unique beer style emerged several hundred years ago, and it remains so today. It is very pale, lightly fruity and crisp–eminently quaffable. According to German law, Kolsch bier is a protected appellation; only beers produced at breweries in the Koln Brewers Union can use the term Kolsch.

If you are interested in learning more about Beer Style Guidelines, go to the Beer Judge Certification Program website at http://www.BJCP.org and click on the "guidelines" link.

A word about regionality–although most beer styles have guidelines to describe how they should look, smell, and taste, very often brewers will exercise their autonomy in their brewhouses creating their own "take" on a given style. In cases like this, all bets are off and standard beer styles guidelines can often be rendered moot.

If you really want to understand a particular beer style, it's always best to taste the beers made by those who brewed original versions of that style. This often means seeking out traditional beer styles from

Germany, Belgium and the UK. Beers made elsewhere are often less-than-authentic copies of the original style.

The Mechanics of Beer Evaluation

When going through the motions of evaluating beer, there is a recommended step-by-step procedure. The reasons for this methodical process are described below. You should assess each of the following in this order:

1) Aroma
2) Appearance
3) Taste
4) Aftertaste
5) Mouthfeel

The aroma should be assessed first because beer aromatics are fleeting; this means they waft off into the air rather quickly. If, for some reason, a beer's aromatics are low or difficult to assess, try swirling the beer (agitate it) to create more head. The carbonation coming out of solution will bring more aromatics with it.

The next assessment of the beer is its appearance. The total appearance consists of the beer's color, clarity and head retention. Each of these is dependent on its style; some beer styles are pale yellow; some are dark brown or black. Similarly, while most beers are very clear, others like Hefeweizen or New England IPA are expected to be hazy or even opaque. Lastly, some beer styles exhibit very little head, while others often throw a billowing head.

Assessing a beer's taste is a matter of noting the various flavor nuances in the beer. Not only do the ingredients play a role in the beer's taste (barley, wheat, hops, etc.), but so does the effect and result of yeast and fermentation (fruitiness, alcohol, etc.). Flavor assessment can often be done by dividing the flavor impression into foretaste and mid-taste; different ingredients in the beer can be more amplified depending on where on the tongue they are tasted.

Despite decades of negative marketing to the contrary, beer is *supposed to* have aftertaste. It's in the aftertaste that all the ingredients in the beer come together in balance and harmony. If a single ingredient dominates the aftertaste (also referred to as the finish), then balance and harmony are not achieved, and the overall assessment of the beer may not be a positive one. Many people agree that it's the aftertaste of a beer that encourages to you have another one, or not.

One aspect of beer evaluation that is often overlooked is that of "mouthfeel." This is literally the feel of the beer on the palate. Mouthfeel may include the prickly effects of carbonation, the body (thickness or viscosity), astringency from dark grain or hop bitterness and alcohol warmth. Mouthfeel can have a great effect on the overall appeal of a beer and it should not be overlooked.

Parameters of Style

As you explore the wide world of beer styles, you're likely to notice that a lot of breweries include some peculiar information on their packaging; you might even see some of this same info on the menu at your local brewery tap room or bottle shop. Listed along with the names and styles of the beer there is often information regarding the beers' color, bitterness and alcohol content. These are expressed in "IBUs", "SRMs" and "ABVs".

IBU stands for *International Bittering Units*, and this is a numerical way of telling the consumer the level of perceived bitterness in the beer. Some beer styles that are not intended to be notably bitter will have an IBU rating that is in the teens or 20's. Other beers styles, such as IPAs, that are intended to be more bitter will have IBU ratings in the 60's or 70's". Occasionally you may trip across a beer that claims to have an IBU rating of 90 or 100+, but this is mostly braggadocio since the human palate cannot discern bitterness levels over 80 IBU or so.

SRM stands for *Standard Reference Method*, which is just a fancy way of expressing beer color. The spectrum of earth tones that covers all beers –from pale yellow to opaque black and everything in between—have been given numerical values from 1 to 40 (40 being the darkest). Useless factoid: beer color on the SRM scale is measured with an instrument called a spectrophotometer.

ABV stands for *Alcohol by Volume*. This is a measure of the alcohol content of any given beverage. The average ABV in beer for many years hovered around 5 or 5.5%; now it seems that number has gradually crept up to 6 or 7%. Don't be surprised to find certain beer styles that routinely tip the ABV scale at up to 12 or 14%!

Since all beers have color, bitterness and alcohol content, and these are all scientifically measurable, IBU, SRM and ABV have become the three cornerstones (or parameters) of all beer styles. These parameters help identify and differentiate the multitude of beer styles that exist in the world.

About the Review Sheet

The review sheets that comprise the remainder of this book were designed by me to be useful to both novice and expert alike. The top section is simply the factual information about the beer that should be easily obtainable from the bar, brewery, or bottle itself.

The next section is subjective, as there are no right or wrong answers. But it gives you an opportunity to slow down and really think about what is going on. For each characteristic, I like to jot down my impressions and then rate each one, from 1 to 5. Beginners will notice how quickly they improve in this area over time if you really focus and take notes at each tasting session.

Next I left a section on possible food pairings, as the idea of pairing beers with food is a rapidly growing phenomenon, much like we have seen with wine pairings for decades.

The final section is one that I use to write about the experience of tasting that particular beer so I can remember it in the future. Was I at home, at a local brewery, or on vacation? Did I drink it out of a bottle or was it on draft? Was there a special occasion involved? Who was I with and what did they think of the beer(s) we tasted? It may seem like extraneous information, but as your journal fills up with dozens of beers, you'll be glad that you included it.

Thank you for purchasing my journal and I wish you the best on your beer-tasting journey.

Cheers!

Marty Nachel
Chicago, Illinois
September 2019

ABOUT THE AUTHOR

Over the past 35 years, Marty Nachel has been involved in the beer industry in many capacities, including Beer Writer, Beer Judge and Beer Educator.

His books include *Beer Across America, Beer for Dummies,* and *Homebrewing for Dummies*.

He has judged professionally at the Great American Beer Festival, the World Beer Cup, Festival of Barrel Aged Beer and Copa Cervezas de America in Santiago, Chile.

As a beer educator, he is on the Advisory Board for College of DuPage Business of Craft Beer certificate program, where he also teaches the program's two prerequisite introductory classes.

Most recently Marty earned Draught Master status at the Heineken brewery in Amsterdam and he does quality training on behalf of the Heineken brand.

Just for fun he has visited over 500 breweries on three continents.

You can check out Marty's web page at: http://www.NachelBeerEducation.com or visit him on Skillshare at: https://www.skillshare.com/user/nachel to take one of his online classes.

Beer Name

Brewery _____ Style _____

ABV _____ IBU _____ OG _____

Appearance		☆ ☆ ☆ ☆ ☆
Aroma		☆ ☆ ☆ ☆ ☆
Body		☆ ☆ ☆ ☆ ☆
Taste		☆ ☆ ☆ ☆ ☆
Finish		☆ ☆ ☆ ☆ ☆

Pairs With	Serving Temperature

Notes

Ratings ☆ ☆ ☆ ☆ ☆

Beer Name

Brewery _____ Style _____

ABV _____ IBU _____ OG _____

Appearance		☆ ☆ ☆ ☆ ☆
Aroma		☆ ☆ ☆ ☆ ☆
Body		☆ ☆ ☆ ☆ ☆
Taste		☆ ☆ ☆ ☆ ☆
Finish		☆ ☆ ☆ ☆ ☆

Pairs With	Serving Temperature

Notes

Ratings ☆ ☆ ☆ ☆ ☆

Beer Name

Brewery _____   Style _____

ABV _____   IBU _____   OG _____

Appearance		☆ ☆ ☆ ☆ ☆
Aroma		☆ ☆ ☆ ☆ ☆
Body		☆ ☆ ☆ ☆ ☆
Taste		☆ ☆ ☆ ☆ ☆
Finish		☆ ☆ ☆ ☆ ☆

Pairs With	Serving Temperature

Notes

Ratings ☆ ☆ ☆ ☆ ☆

Beer Name

Brewery _____ Style _____

ABV _____ IBU _____ OG _____

Appearance		☆ ☆ ☆ ☆ ☆
Aroma		☆ ☆ ☆ ☆ ☆
Body		☆ ☆ ☆ ☆ ☆
Taste		☆ ☆ ☆ ☆ ☆
Finish		☆ ☆ ☆ ☆ ☆

Pairs With	Serving Temperature

Notes

Ratings ☆ ☆ ☆ ☆ ☆

Beer Name

Brewery _____ Style _____

ABV _____ IBU _____ OG _____

Appearance		☆ ☆ ☆ ☆ ☆
Aroma		☆ ☆ ☆ ☆ ☆
Body		☆ ☆ ☆ ☆ ☆
Taste		☆ ☆ ☆ ☆ ☆
Finish		☆ ☆ ☆ ☆ ☆

Pairs With	Serving Temperature

Notes

Ratings ☆ ☆ ☆ ☆ ☆

Beer Name

Brewery	Style
ABV	IBU	OG

Appearance		☆ ☆ ☆ ☆ ☆
Aroma		☆ ☆ ☆ ☆ ☆
Body		☆ ☆ ☆ ☆ ☆
Taste		☆ ☆ ☆ ☆ ☆
Finish		☆ ☆ ☆ ☆ ☆

Pairs With	Serving Temperature

Notes

Ratings ☆ ☆ ☆ ☆ ☆

Beer Name

Brewery _____ Style _____

ABV _____ IBU _____ OG _____

Appearance		☆ ☆ ☆ ☆ ☆
Aroma		☆ ☆ ☆ ☆ ☆
Body		☆ ☆ ☆ ☆ ☆
Taste		☆ ☆ ☆ ☆ ☆
Finish		☆ ☆ ☆ ☆ ☆

Pairs With	Serving Temperature

Notes

Ratings ☆ ☆ ☆ ☆ ☆

Beer Name

Brewery	Style	
ABV	IBU	OG

Appearance		☆ ☆ ☆ ☆ ☆
Aroma		☆ ☆ ☆ ☆ ☆
Body		☆ ☆ ☆ ☆ ☆
Taste		☆ ☆ ☆ ☆ ☆
Finish		☆ ☆ ☆ ☆ ☆

Pairs With	Serving Temperature

Notes

Ratings ☆ ☆ ☆ ☆ ☆

Beer Name

Brewery _____ Style _____

ABV _____ IBU _____ OG _____

Appearance		☆ ☆ ☆ ☆ ☆
Aroma		☆ ☆ ☆ ☆ ☆
Body		☆ ☆ ☆ ☆ ☆
Taste		☆ ☆ ☆ ☆ ☆
Finish		☆ ☆ ☆ ☆ ☆

Pairs With	Serving Temperature

Notes

Ratings ☆ ☆ ☆ ☆ ☆

Beer Name

Brewery	Style	
ABV	IBU	OG

Appearance		☆ ☆ ☆ ☆ ☆
Aroma		☆ ☆ ☆ ☆ ☆
Body		☆ ☆ ☆ ☆ ☆
Taste		☆ ☆ ☆ ☆ ☆
Finish		☆ ☆ ☆ ☆ ☆

Pairs With	Serving Temperature

Notes

Ratings ☆ ☆ ☆ ☆ ☆

Beer Name

Brewery _____ Style _____

ABV _____ IBU _____ OG _____

Appearance		☆ ☆ ☆ ☆ ☆
Aroma		☆ ☆ ☆ ☆ ☆
Body		☆ ☆ ☆ ☆ ☆
Taste		☆ ☆ ☆ ☆ ☆
Finish		☆ ☆ ☆ ☆ ☆

Pairs With	Serving Temperature

Notes

Ratings ☆ ☆ ☆ ☆ ☆

Beer Name

Brewery	Style	
ABV	IBU	OG

Appearance		☆ ☆ ☆ ☆ ☆
Aroma		☆ ☆ ☆ ☆ ☆
Body		☆ ☆ ☆ ☆ ☆
Taste		☆ ☆ ☆ ☆ ☆
Finish		☆ ☆ ☆ ☆ ☆

Pairs With	Serving Temperature

Notes

Ratings ☆ ☆ ☆ ☆ ☆

Beer Name

Brewery	Style
ABV	IBU	OG

Appearance		☆ ☆ ☆ ☆ ☆
Aroma		☆ ☆ ☆ ☆ ☆
Body		☆ ☆ ☆ ☆ ☆
Taste		☆ ☆ ☆ ☆ ☆
Finish		☆ ☆ ☆ ☆ ☆

Pairs With	Serving Temperature

Notes

Ratings ☆ ☆ ☆ ☆ ☆

Beer Name

Brewery _____   Style _____

ABV _____   IBU _____   OG _____

Appearance		☆ ☆ ☆ ☆ ☆
Aroma		☆ ☆ ☆ ☆ ☆
Body		☆ ☆ ☆ ☆ ☆
Taste		☆ ☆ ☆ ☆ ☆
Finish		☆ ☆ ☆ ☆ ☆

Pairs With	Serving Temperature

Notes

Ratings ☆ ☆ ☆ ☆ ☆

Beer Name

Brewery _____   Style _____

ABV _____   IBU _____   OG _____

Appearance		☆ ☆ ☆ ☆ ☆
Aroma		☆ ☆ ☆ ☆ ☆
Body		☆ ☆ ☆ ☆ ☆
Taste		☆ ☆ ☆ ☆ ☆
Finish		☆ ☆ ☆ ☆ ☆

Pairs With	Serving Temperature

Notes

Ratings ☆ ☆ ☆ ☆ ☆

Beer Name

Brewery	Style

ABV   IBU   OG

Appearance		☆ ☆ ☆ ☆ ☆
Aroma		☆ ☆ ☆ ☆ ☆
Body		☆ ☆ ☆ ☆ ☆
Taste		☆ ☆ ☆ ☆ ☆
Finish		☆ ☆ ☆ ☆ ☆

Pairs With	Serving Temperature

Notes

Ratings ☆ ☆ ☆ ☆ ☆

Beer Name

Brewery	Style
ABV	IBU	OG

Appearance		☆ ☆ ☆ ☆ ☆
Aroma		☆ ☆ ☆ ☆ ☆
Body		☆ ☆ ☆ ☆ ☆
Taste		☆ ☆ ☆ ☆ ☆
Finish		☆ ☆ ☆ ☆ ☆

Pairs With	Serving Temperature

Notes

Ratings ☆ ☆ ☆ ☆ ☆

Beer Name

Brewery _____ Style _____

ABV _____ IBU _____ OG _____

Appearance		☆ ☆ ☆ ☆ ☆
Aroma		☆ ☆ ☆ ☆ ☆
Body		☆ ☆ ☆ ☆ ☆
Taste		☆ ☆ ☆ ☆ ☆
Finish		☆ ☆ ☆ ☆ ☆

Pairs With	Serving Temperature

Notes

Ratings ☆ ☆ ☆ ☆ ☆

Beer Name

Brewery	Style	
ABV	IBU	OG

Appearance		☆ ☆ ☆ ☆ ☆
Aroma		☆ ☆ ☆ ☆ ☆
Body		☆ ☆ ☆ ☆ ☆
Taste		☆ ☆ ☆ ☆ ☆
Finish		☆ ☆ ☆ ☆ ☆

Pairs With	Serving Temperature

Notes

Ratings ☆ ☆ ☆ ☆ ☆

Beer Name

Brewery _____ Style _____

ABV _____ IBU _____ OG _____

Appearance		☆ ☆ ☆ ☆ ☆
Aroma		☆ ☆ ☆ ☆ ☆
Body		☆ ☆ ☆ ☆ ☆
Taste		☆ ☆ ☆ ☆ ☆
Finish		☆ ☆ ☆ ☆ ☆

Pairs With	Serving Temperature

Notes

Ratings ☆ ☆ ☆ ☆ ☆

Beer Name

Brewery	Style	
ABV	IBU	OG

Appearance		☆ ☆ ☆ ☆ ☆
Aroma		☆ ☆ ☆ ☆ ☆
Body		☆ ☆ ☆ ☆ ☆
Taste		☆ ☆ ☆ ☆ ☆
Finish		☆ ☆ ☆ ☆ ☆

Pairs With	Serving Temperature

Notes

Ratings ☆ ☆ ☆ ☆ ☆

Beer Name

Brewery _____   Style _____

ABV _____   IBU _____   OG _____

Appearance		☆ ☆ ☆ ☆ ☆
Aroma		☆ ☆ ☆ ☆ ☆
Body		☆ ☆ ☆ ☆ ☆
Taste		☆ ☆ ☆ ☆ ☆
Finish		☆ ☆ ☆ ☆ ☆

Pairs With	Serving Temperature

Notes

Ratings ☆ ☆ ☆ ☆ ☆

Beer Name

Brewery _____ Style _____

ABV _____ IBU _____ OG _____

Appearance		☆ ☆ ☆ ☆ ☆
Aroma		☆ ☆ ☆ ☆ ☆
Body		☆ ☆ ☆ ☆ ☆
Taste		☆ ☆ ☆ ☆ ☆
Finish		☆ ☆ ☆ ☆ ☆

Pairs With	Serving Temperature

Notes

Ratings ☆ ☆ ☆ ☆ ☆

Beer Name

Brewery _____   Style _____

ABV _____   IBU _____   OG _____

Appearance		☆ ☆ ☆ ☆ ☆
Aroma		☆ ☆ ☆ ☆ ☆
Body		☆ ☆ ☆ ☆ ☆
Taste		☆ ☆ ☆ ☆ ☆
Finish		☆ ☆ ☆ ☆ ☆

Pairs With	Serving Temperature

Notes

Ratings ☆ ☆ ☆ ☆ ☆

Beer Name

Brewery   Style

ABV   IBU   OG

Appearance		☆ ☆ ☆ ☆ ☆
Aroma		☆ ☆ ☆ ☆ ☆
Body		☆ ☆ ☆ ☆ ☆
Taste		☆ ☆ ☆ ☆ ☆
Finish		☆ ☆ ☆ ☆ ☆

Pairs With	Serving Temperature

Notes

Ratings ☆ ☆ ☆ ☆ ☆

Beer Name

Brewery	Style
ABV	IBU	OG

Appearance		☆ ☆ ☆ ☆ ☆
Aroma		☆ ☆ ☆ ☆ ☆
Body		☆ ☆ ☆ ☆ ☆
Taste		☆ ☆ ☆ ☆ ☆
Finish		☆ ☆ ☆ ☆ ☆

Pairs With	Serving Temperature

Notes

Ratings ☆ ☆ ☆ ☆ ☆

Beer Name

Brewery _____ Style _____

ABV _____ IBU _____ OG _____

Appearance		☆ ☆ ☆ ☆ ☆
Aroma		☆ ☆ ☆ ☆ ☆
Body		☆ ☆ ☆ ☆ ☆
Taste		☆ ☆ ☆ ☆ ☆
Finish		☆ ☆ ☆ ☆ ☆

Pairs With	Serving Temperature

Notes

Ratings ☆ ☆ ☆ ☆ ☆

Beer Name

Brewery _____   Style _____

ABV _____   IBU _____   OG _____

Appearance		☆ ☆ ☆ ☆ ☆
Aroma		☆ ☆ ☆ ☆ ☆
Body		☆ ☆ ☆ ☆ ☆
Taste		☆ ☆ ☆ ☆ ☆
Finish		☆ ☆ ☆ ☆ ☆

Pairs With	Serving Temperature

Notes

Ratings ☆ ☆ ☆ ☆ ☆

Beer Name

Brewery _____ Style _____

ABV _____ IBU _____ OG _____

Appearance		☆ ☆ ☆ ☆ ☆
Aroma		☆ ☆ ☆ ☆ ☆
Body		☆ ☆ ☆ ☆ ☆
Taste		☆ ☆ ☆ ☆ ☆
Finish		☆ ☆ ☆ ☆ ☆

Pairs With	Serving Temperature

Notes

Ratings ☆ ☆ ☆ ☆ ☆

Beer Name

Brewery _____   Style _____

ABV _____   IBU _____   OG _____

Appearance		☆ ☆ ☆ ☆ ☆
Aroma		☆ ☆ ☆ ☆ ☆
Body		☆ ☆ ☆ ☆ ☆
Taste		☆ ☆ ☆ ☆ ☆
Finish		☆ ☆ ☆ ☆ ☆

Pairs With	Serving Temperature

Notes

Ratings ☆ ☆ ☆ ☆ ☆

Beer Name

Brewery _____ Style _____

ABV _____ IBU _____ OG _____

Appearance		☆ ☆ ☆ ☆ ☆
Aroma		☆ ☆ ☆ ☆ ☆
Body		☆ ☆ ☆ ☆ ☆
Taste		☆ ☆ ☆ ☆ ☆
Finish		☆ ☆ ☆ ☆ ☆

Pairs With	Serving Temperature

Notes

Ratings ☆ ☆ ☆ ☆ ☆

Beer Name

Brewery _____ Style _____

ABV _____ IBU _____ OG _____

Appearance		☆ ☆ ☆ ☆ ☆
Aroma		☆ ☆ ☆ ☆ ☆
Body		☆ ☆ ☆ ☆ ☆
Taste		☆ ☆ ☆ ☆ ☆
Finish		☆ ☆ ☆ ☆ ☆

Pairs With	Serving Temperature

Notes

Ratings ☆ ☆ ☆ ☆ ☆

Beer Name

Brewery _____ Style _____

ABV _____ IBU _____ OG _____

Appearance		☆ ☆ ☆ ☆ ☆
Aroma		☆ ☆ ☆ ☆ ☆
Body		☆ ☆ ☆ ☆ ☆
Taste		☆ ☆ ☆ ☆ ☆
Finish		☆ ☆ ☆ ☆ ☆

Pairs With	Serving Temperature

Notes

Ratings ☆ ☆ ☆ ☆ ☆

Beer Name

Brewery	Style	
ABV	IBU	OG

Appearance		☆ ☆ ☆ ☆ ☆
Aroma		☆ ☆ ☆ ☆ ☆
Body		☆ ☆ ☆ ☆ ☆
Taste		☆ ☆ ☆ ☆ ☆
Finish		☆ ☆ ☆ ☆ ☆

Pairs With	Serving Temperature

Notes

Ratings ☆ ☆ ☆ ☆ ☆

Beer Name

Brewery _____   Style _____

ABV _____   IBU _____   OG _____

Appearance		☆ ☆ ☆ ☆ ☆
Aroma		☆ ☆ ☆ ☆ ☆
Body		☆ ☆ ☆ ☆ ☆
Taste		☆ ☆ ☆ ☆ ☆
Finish		☆ ☆ ☆ ☆ ☆

Pairs With	Serving Temperature

Notes

Ratings ☆ ☆ ☆ ☆ ☆

Beer Name

Brewery _____ Style _____

ABV _____ IBU _____ OG _____

Appearance		☆ ☆ ☆ ☆ ☆
Aroma		☆ ☆ ☆ ☆ ☆
Body		☆ ☆ ☆ ☆ ☆
Taste		☆ ☆ ☆ ☆ ☆
Finish		☆ ☆ ☆ ☆ ☆

Pairs With	Serving Temperature

Notes

Ratings ☆ ☆ ☆ ☆ ☆

Beer Name

Brewery _____ Style _____

ABV _____ IBU _____ OG _____

Appearance		☆ ☆ ☆ ☆ ☆
Aroma		☆ ☆ ☆ ☆ ☆
Body		☆ ☆ ☆ ☆ ☆
Taste		☆ ☆ ☆ ☆ ☆
Finish		☆ ☆ ☆ ☆ ☆

Pairs With	Serving Temperature

Notes

Ratings ☆ ☆ ☆ ☆ ☆

Beer Name

Brewery _____ Style _____

ABV _____ IBU _____ OG _____

Appearance		☆ ☆ ☆ ☆ ☆
Aroma		☆ ☆ ☆ ☆ ☆
Body		☆ ☆ ☆ ☆ ☆
Taste		☆ ☆ ☆ ☆ ☆
Finish		☆ ☆ ☆ ☆ ☆

Pairs With	Serving Temperature

Notes

Ratings ☆ ☆ ☆ ☆ ☆

Beer Name

Brewery _____ Style _____

ABV _____ IBU _____ OG _____

Appearance		☆ ☆ ☆ ☆ ☆
Aroma		☆ ☆ ☆ ☆ ☆
Body		☆ ☆ ☆ ☆ ☆
Taste		☆ ☆ ☆ ☆ ☆
Finish		☆ ☆ ☆ ☆ ☆

Pairs With	Serving Temperature

Notes

Ratings ☆ ☆ ☆ ☆ ☆

Beer Name

Brewery _____ Style _____

ABV _____ IBU _____ OG _____

Appearance		☆ ☆ ☆ ☆ ☆
Aroma		☆ ☆ ☆ ☆ ☆
Body		☆ ☆ ☆ ☆ ☆
Taste		☆ ☆ ☆ ☆ ☆
Finish		☆ ☆ ☆ ☆ ☆

Pairs With	Serving Temperature

Notes

Ratings ☆ ☆ ☆ ☆ ☆

Beer Name

Brewery _____   Style _____

ABV _____   IBU _____   OG _____

Appearance		☆ ☆ ☆ ☆ ☆
Aroma		☆ ☆ ☆ ☆ ☆
Body		☆ ☆ ☆ ☆ ☆
Taste		☆ ☆ ☆ ☆ ☆
Finish		☆ ☆ ☆ ☆ ☆

Pairs With	Serving Temperature

Notes

Ratings ☆ ☆ ☆ ☆ ☆

Beer Name

Brewery _____ Style _____

ABV _____ IBU _____ OG _____

Appearance		☆ ☆ ☆ ☆ ☆
Aroma		☆ ☆ ☆ ☆ ☆
Body		☆ ☆ ☆ ☆ ☆
Taste		☆ ☆ ☆ ☆ ☆
Finish		☆ ☆ ☆ ☆ ☆

Pairs With	Serving Temperature

Notes

Ratings ☆ ☆ ☆ ☆ ☆

Beer Name

Brewery _____ Style _____

ABV _____ IBU _____ OG _____

Appearance		☆ ☆ ☆ ☆ ☆
Aroma		☆ ☆ ☆ ☆ ☆
Body		☆ ☆ ☆ ☆ ☆
Taste		☆ ☆ ☆ ☆ ☆
Finish		☆ ☆ ☆ ☆ ☆

Pairs With	Serving Temperature

Notes

Ratings ☆ ☆ ☆ ☆ ☆

Beer Name

Brewery _____ Style _____

ABV _____ IBU _____ OG _____

Appearance		☆ ☆ ☆ ☆ ☆
Aroma		☆ ☆ ☆ ☆ ☆
Body		☆ ☆ ☆ ☆ ☆
Taste		☆ ☆ ☆ ☆ ☆
Finish		☆ ☆ ☆ ☆ ☆

Pairs With	Serving Temperature

Notes

Ratings ☆ ☆ ☆ ☆ ☆

Beer Name

Brewery _____   Style _____

ABV _____   IBU _____   OG _____

Appearance		☆ ☆ ☆ ☆ ☆
Aroma		☆ ☆ ☆ ☆ ☆
Body		☆ ☆ ☆ ☆ ☆
Taste		☆ ☆ ☆ ☆ ☆
Finish		☆ ☆ ☆ ☆ ☆

Pairs With	Serving Temperature

Notes

Ratings ☆ ☆ ☆ ☆ ☆

Beer Name

Brewery _____ Style _____

ABV _____ IBU _____ OG _____

Appearance		☆ ☆ ☆ ☆ ☆
Aroma		☆ ☆ ☆ ☆ ☆
Body		☆ ☆ ☆ ☆ ☆
Taste		☆ ☆ ☆ ☆ ☆
Finish		☆ ☆ ☆ ☆ ☆

Pairs With	Serving Temperature

Notes

Ratings ☆ ☆ ☆ ☆ ☆

Beer Name

Brewery _____ Style _____

ABV _____ IBU _____ OG _____

Appearance		☆ ☆ ☆ ☆ ☆
Aroma		☆ ☆ ☆ ☆ ☆
Body		☆ ☆ ☆ ☆ ☆
Taste		☆ ☆ ☆ ☆ ☆
Finish		☆ ☆ ☆ ☆ ☆

Pairs With	Serving Temperature

Notes

Ratings ☆ ☆ ☆ ☆ ☆

Beer Name

Brewery _____ Style _____

ABV _____ IBU _____ OG _____

Appearance		☆ ☆ ☆ ☆ ☆
Aroma		☆ ☆ ☆ ☆ ☆
Body		☆ ☆ ☆ ☆ ☆
Taste		☆ ☆ ☆ ☆ ☆
Finish		☆ ☆ ☆ ☆ ☆

Pairs With	Serving Temperature

Notes

Ratings ☆ ☆ ☆ ☆ ☆

Beer Name

Brewery _____ Style _____

ABV _____ IBU _____ OG _____

Appearance		☆ ☆ ☆ ☆ ☆
Aroma		☆ ☆ ☆ ☆ ☆
Body		☆ ☆ ☆ ☆ ☆
Taste		☆ ☆ ☆ ☆ ☆
Finish		☆ ☆ ☆ ☆ ☆

Pairs With	Serving Temperature

Notes

Ratings ☆ ☆ ☆ ☆ ☆

Beer Name

Brewery _____ Style _____

ABV _____ IBU _____ OG _____

Appearance		☆ ☆ ☆ ☆ ☆
Aroma		☆ ☆ ☆ ☆ ☆
Body		☆ ☆ ☆ ☆ ☆
Taste		☆ ☆ ☆ ☆ ☆
Finish		☆ ☆ ☆ ☆ ☆

Pairs With	Serving Temperature

Notes

Ratings ☆ ☆ ☆ ☆ ☆

Beer Name

Brewery _____   Style _____

ABV _____   IBU _____   OG _____

Appearance		☆ ☆ ☆ ☆ ☆
Aroma		☆ ☆ ☆ ☆ ☆
Body		☆ ☆ ☆ ☆ ☆
Taste		☆ ☆ ☆ ☆ ☆
Finish		☆ ☆ ☆ ☆ ☆

Pairs With	Serving Temperature

Notes

Ratings ☆ ☆ ☆ ☆ ☆

Beer Name

Brewery _____ Style _____

ABV _____ IBU _____ OG _____

Appearance		☆ ☆ ☆ ☆ ☆
Aroma		☆ ☆ ☆ ☆ ☆
Body		☆ ☆ ☆ ☆ ☆
Taste		☆ ☆ ☆ ☆ ☆
Finish		☆ ☆ ☆ ☆ ☆

Pairs With	Serving Temperature

Notes

Ratings ☆ ☆ ☆ ☆ ☆

Beer Name

Brewery _____ Style _____

ABV _____ IBU _____ OG _____

Appearance		☆ ☆ ☆ ☆ ☆
Aroma		☆ ☆ ☆ ☆ ☆
Body		☆ ☆ ☆ ☆ ☆
Taste		☆ ☆ ☆ ☆ ☆
Finish		☆ ☆ ☆ ☆ ☆

Pairs With	Serving Temperature

Notes

Ratings ☆ ☆ ☆ ☆ ☆

Beer Name

Brewery _____ Style _____

ABV _____ IBU _____ OG _____

Appearance		☆ ☆ ☆ ☆ ☆
Aroma		☆ ☆ ☆ ☆ ☆
Body		☆ ☆ ☆ ☆ ☆
Taste		☆ ☆ ☆ ☆ ☆
Finish		☆ ☆ ☆ ☆ ☆

Pairs With	Serving Temperature

Notes

Ratings ☆ ☆ ☆ ☆ ☆

Beer Name

Brewery _____ Style _____

ABV _____ IBU _____ OG _____

Appearance		☆ ☆ ☆ ☆ ☆
Aroma		☆ ☆ ☆ ☆ ☆
Body		☆ ☆ ☆ ☆ ☆
Taste		☆ ☆ ☆ ☆ ☆
Finish		☆ ☆ ☆ ☆ ☆

Pairs With	Serving Temperature

Notes

Ratings ☆ ☆ ☆ ☆ ☆

Beer Name

Brewery _____ Style _____

ABV _____ IBU _____ OG _____

Appearance		☆ ☆ ☆ ☆ ☆
Aroma		☆ ☆ ☆ ☆ ☆
Body		☆ ☆ ☆ ☆ ☆
Taste		☆ ☆ ☆ ☆ ☆
Finish		☆ ☆ ☆ ☆ ☆

Pairs With	Serving Temperature

Notes

Ratings ☆ ☆ ☆ ☆ ☆

Beer Name

Brewery _____ Style _____

ABV _____ IBU _____ OG _____

Appearance		☆ ☆ ☆ ☆ ☆
Aroma		☆ ☆ ☆ ☆ ☆
Body		☆ ☆ ☆ ☆ ☆
Taste		☆ ☆ ☆ ☆ ☆
Finish		☆ ☆ ☆ ☆ ☆

Pairs With	Serving Temperature

Notes

Ratings ☆ ☆ ☆ ☆ ☆

Beer Name

Brewery _____ Style _____

ABV _____ IBU _____ OG _____

Appearance		☆ ☆ ☆ ☆ ☆
Aroma		☆ ☆ ☆ ☆ ☆
Body		☆ ☆ ☆ ☆ ☆
Taste		☆ ☆ ☆ ☆ ☆
Finish		☆ ☆ ☆ ☆ ☆

Pairs With	Serving Temperature

Notes

Ratings ☆ ☆ ☆ ☆ ☆

Beer Name

Brewery _____ Style _____

ABV _____ IBU _____ OG _____

Appearance		☆ ☆ ☆ ☆ ☆
Aroma		☆ ☆ ☆ ☆ ☆
Body		☆ ☆ ☆ ☆ ☆
Taste		☆ ☆ ☆ ☆ ☆
Finish		☆ ☆ ☆ ☆ ☆

Pairs With	Serving Temperature

Notes

Ratings ☆ ☆ ☆ ☆ ☆

Beer Name

Brewery _____ Style _____

ABV _____ IBU _____ OG _____

Appearance		☆ ☆ ☆ ☆ ☆
Aroma		☆ ☆ ☆ ☆ ☆
Body		☆ ☆ ☆ ☆ ☆
Taste		☆ ☆ ☆ ☆ ☆
Finish		☆ ☆ ☆ ☆ ☆

Pairs With	Serving Temperature

Notes

Ratings ☆ ☆ ☆ ☆ ☆

Beer Name

Brewery	Style
ABV	IBU	OG

Appearance		☆ ☆ ☆ ☆ ☆
Aroma		☆ ☆ ☆ ☆ ☆
Body		☆ ☆ ☆ ☆ ☆
Taste		☆ ☆ ☆ ☆ ☆
Finish		☆ ☆ ☆ ☆ ☆

Pairs With	Serving Temperature

Notes

Ratings ☆ ☆ ☆ ☆ ☆

Beer Name		
Brewery	Style	
ABV	IBU	OG

Appearance		☆ ☆ ☆ ☆ ☆
Aroma		☆ ☆ ☆ ☆ ☆
Body		☆ ☆ ☆ ☆ ☆
Taste		☆ ☆ ☆ ☆ ☆
Finish		☆ ☆ ☆ ☆ ☆

Pairs With	Serving Temperature

Notes

Ratings ☆ ☆ ☆ ☆ ☆

Beer Name

Brewery _____   Style _____

ABV _____   IBU _____   OG _____

Appearance		☆ ☆ ☆ ☆ ☆
Aroma		☆ ☆ ☆ ☆ ☆
Body		☆ ☆ ☆ ☆ ☆
Taste		☆ ☆ ☆ ☆ ☆
Finish		☆ ☆ ☆ ☆ ☆

Pairs With	Serving Temperature

Notes

Ratings ☆ ☆ ☆ ☆ ☆

Beer Name

Brewery _____ Style _____

ABV _____ IBU _____ OG _____

Appearance		☆ ☆ ☆ ☆ ☆
Aroma		☆ ☆ ☆ ☆ ☆
Body		☆ ☆ ☆ ☆ ☆
Taste		☆ ☆ ☆ ☆ ☆
Finish		☆ ☆ ☆ ☆ ☆

Pairs With	Serving Temperature

Notes

Ratings ☆ ☆ ☆ ☆ ☆

Beer Name

Brewery _____ Style _____

ABV _____ IBU _____ OG _____

Appearance		☆ ☆ ☆ ☆ ☆
Aroma		☆ ☆ ☆ ☆ ☆
Body		☆ ☆ ☆ ☆ ☆
Taste		☆ ☆ ☆ ☆ ☆
Finish		☆ ☆ ☆ ☆ ☆

Pairs With	Serving Temperature

Notes

Ratings ☆ ☆ ☆ ☆ ☆

Beer Name

Brewery _____ Style _____

ABV _____ IBU _____ OG _____

Appearance		☆ ☆ ☆ ☆ ☆
Aroma		☆ ☆ ☆ ☆ ☆
Body		☆ ☆ ☆ ☆ ☆
Taste		☆ ☆ ☆ ☆ ☆
Finish		☆ ☆ ☆ ☆ ☆

Pairs With	Serving Temperature

Notes

Ratings ☆ ☆ ☆ ☆ ☆

Beer Name

Brewery _____ Style _____

ABV _____ IBU _____ OG _____

Appearance		☆ ☆ ☆ ☆ ☆
Aroma		☆ ☆ ☆ ☆ ☆
Body		☆ ☆ ☆ ☆ ☆
Taste		☆ ☆ ☆ ☆ ☆
Finish		☆ ☆ ☆ ☆ ☆

Pairs With	Serving Temperature

Notes

Ratings ☆ ☆ ☆ ☆ ☆

Beer Name	
Brewery	Style
ABV	IBU	OG

Appearance		☆ ☆ ☆ ☆ ☆
Aroma		☆ ☆ ☆ ☆ ☆
Body		☆ ☆ ☆ ☆ ☆
Taste		☆ ☆ ☆ ☆ ☆
Finish		☆ ☆ ☆ ☆ ☆

Pairs With	Serving Temperature

Notes

Ratings ☆ ☆ ☆ ☆ ☆

Beer Name

Brewery _____   Style _____

ABV _____   IBU _____   OG _____

Appearance		☆ ☆ ☆ ☆ ☆
Aroma		☆ ☆ ☆ ☆ ☆
Body		☆ ☆ ☆ ☆ ☆
Taste		☆ ☆ ☆ ☆ ☆
Finish		☆ ☆ ☆ ☆ ☆

Pairs With	Serving Temperature

Notes

Ratings ☆ ☆ ☆ ☆ ☆

Beer Name

Brewery _____ Style _____

ABV _____ IBU _____ OG _____

Appearance		☆ ☆ ☆ ☆ ☆
Aroma		☆ ☆ ☆ ☆ ☆
Body		☆ ☆ ☆ ☆ ☆
Taste		☆ ☆ ☆ ☆ ☆
Finish		☆ ☆ ☆ ☆ ☆

Pairs With	Serving Temperature

Notes

Ratings ☆ ☆ ☆ ☆ ☆

Beer Name

Brewery _____   Style _____

ABV _____   IBU _____   OG _____

Appearance		☆ ☆ ☆ ☆ ☆
Aroma		☆ ☆ ☆ ☆ ☆
Body		☆ ☆ ☆ ☆ ☆
Taste		☆ ☆ ☆ ☆ ☆
Finish		☆ ☆ ☆ ☆ ☆

Pairs With	Serving Temperature

Notes

Ratings ☆ ☆ ☆ ☆ ☆

Beer Name

Brewery _____ Style _____

ABV _____ IBU _____ OG _____

Appearance		☆ ☆ ☆ ☆ ☆
Aroma		☆ ☆ ☆ ☆ ☆
Body		☆ ☆ ☆ ☆ ☆
Taste		☆ ☆ ☆ ☆ ☆
Finish		☆ ☆ ☆ ☆ ☆

Pairs With	Serving Temperature

Notes

Ratings ☆ ☆ ☆ ☆ ☆

Beer Name

Brewery _____ Style _____

ABV _____ IBU _____ OG _____

Appearance		☆ ☆ ☆ ☆ ☆
Aroma		☆ ☆ ☆ ☆ ☆
Body		☆ ☆ ☆ ☆ ☆
Taste		☆ ☆ ☆ ☆ ☆
Finish		☆ ☆ ☆ ☆ ☆

Pairs With	Serving Temperature

Notes

Ratings ☆ ☆ ☆ ☆ ☆

Beer Name

Brewery _____ Style _____

ABV _____ IBU _____ OG _____

Appearance		☆ ☆ ☆ ☆ ☆
Aroma		☆ ☆ ☆ ☆ ☆
Body		☆ ☆ ☆ ☆ ☆
Taste		☆ ☆ ☆ ☆ ☆
Finish		☆ ☆ ☆ ☆ ☆

Pairs With	Serving Temperature

Notes

Ratings ☆ ☆ ☆ ☆ ☆

Beer Name

Brewery _____ Style _____

ABV _____ IBU _____ OG _____

Appearance		☆ ☆ ☆ ☆ ☆
Aroma		☆ ☆ ☆ ☆ ☆
Body		☆ ☆ ☆ ☆ ☆
Taste		☆ ☆ ☆ ☆ ☆
Finish		☆ ☆ ☆ ☆ ☆

Pairs With	Serving Temperature

Notes

Ratings ☆ ☆ ☆ ☆ ☆

Beer Name

Brewery _____ Style _____

ABV _____ IBU _____ OG _____

Appearance		☆ ☆ ☆ ☆ ☆
Aroma		☆ ☆ ☆ ☆ ☆
Body		☆ ☆ ☆ ☆ ☆
Taste		☆ ☆ ☆ ☆ ☆
Finish		☆ ☆ ☆ ☆ ☆

Pairs With	Serving Temperature

Notes

Ratings ☆ ☆ ☆ ☆ ☆

Beer Name

Brewery _____   Style _____

ABV _____   IBU _____   OG _____

Appearance		☆ ☆ ☆ ☆ ☆
Aroma		☆ ☆ ☆ ☆ ☆
Body		☆ ☆ ☆ ☆ ☆
Taste		☆ ☆ ☆ ☆ ☆
Finish		☆ ☆ ☆ ☆ ☆

Pairs With	Serving Temperature

Notes

Ratings ☆ ☆ ☆ ☆ ☆

Beer Name

Brewery _____ Style _____

ABV _____ IBU _____ OG _____

Appearance		☆ ☆ ☆ ☆ ☆
Aroma		☆ ☆ ☆ ☆ ☆
Body		☆ ☆ ☆ ☆ ☆
Taste		☆ ☆ ☆ ☆ ☆
Finish		☆ ☆ ☆ ☆ ☆

Pairs With	Serving Temperature

Notes

Ratings ☆ ☆ ☆ ☆ ☆

Beer Name

Brewery _____   Style _____

ABV _____   IBU _____   OG _____

Appearance		☆ ☆ ☆ ☆ ☆
Aroma		☆ ☆ ☆ ☆ ☆
Body		☆ ☆ ☆ ☆ ☆
Taste		☆ ☆ ☆ ☆ ☆
Finish		☆ ☆ ☆ ☆ ☆

Pairs With	Serving Temperature

Notes

Ratings ☆ ☆ ☆ ☆ ☆

Beer Name

Brewery _____ Style _____

ABV _____ IBU _____ OG _____

Appearance		☆ ☆ ☆ ☆ ☆
Aroma		☆ ☆ ☆ ☆ ☆
Body		☆ ☆ ☆ ☆ ☆
Taste		☆ ☆ ☆ ☆ ☆
Finish		☆ ☆ ☆ ☆ ☆

Pairs With	Serving Temperature

Notes

Ratings ☆ ☆ ☆ ☆ ☆

Beer Name

Brewery _____ Style _____

ABV _____ IBU _____ OG _____

Appearance		☆ ☆ ☆ ☆ ☆
Aroma		☆ ☆ ☆ ☆ ☆
Body		☆ ☆ ☆ ☆ ☆
Taste		☆ ☆ ☆ ☆ ☆
Finish		☆ ☆ ☆ ☆ ☆

Pairs With	Serving Temperature

Notes

Ratings ☆ ☆ ☆ ☆ ☆

Beer Name

Brewery _____ Style _____

ABV _____ IBU _____ OG _____

Appearance		☆ ☆ ☆ ☆ ☆
Aroma		☆ ☆ ☆ ☆ ☆
Body		☆ ☆ ☆ ☆ ☆
Taste		☆ ☆ ☆ ☆ ☆
Finish		☆ ☆ ☆ ☆ ☆

Pairs With	Serving Temperature

Notes

Ratings ☆ ☆ ☆ ☆ ☆

Beer Name

Brewery _____   Style _____

ABV _____   IBU _____   OG _____

Appearance		☆ ☆ ☆ ☆ ☆
Aroma		☆ ☆ ☆ ☆ ☆
Body		☆ ☆ ☆ ☆ ☆
Taste		☆ ☆ ☆ ☆ ☆
Finish		☆ ☆ ☆ ☆ ☆

Pairs With	Serving Temperature

Notes

Ratings ☆ ☆ ☆ ☆ ☆

Beer Name _____

Brewery _____   Style _____

ABV _____   IBU _____   OG _____

Appearance		☆ ☆ ☆ ☆ ☆
Aroma		☆ ☆ ☆ ☆ ☆
Body		☆ ☆ ☆ ☆ ☆
Taste		☆ ☆ ☆ ☆ ☆
Finish		☆ ☆ ☆ ☆ ☆

Pairs With	Serving Temperature

Notes

Ratings ☆ ☆ ☆ ☆ ☆

Beer Name

Brewery _____ Style _____

ABV _____ IBU _____ OG _____

Appearance		☆ ☆ ☆ ☆ ☆
Aroma		☆ ☆ ☆ ☆ ☆
Body		☆ ☆ ☆ ☆ ☆
Taste		☆ ☆ ☆ ☆ ☆
Finish		☆ ☆ ☆ ☆ ☆

Pairs With	Serving Temperature

Notes

Ratings ☆ ☆ ☆ ☆ ☆

Beer Name

Brewery _____ Style _____

ABV _____ IBU _____ OG _____

Appearance		☆ ☆ ☆ ☆ ☆
Aroma		☆ ☆ ☆ ☆ ☆
Body		☆ ☆ ☆ ☆ ☆
Taste		☆ ☆ ☆ ☆ ☆
Finish		☆ ☆ ☆ ☆ ☆

Pairs With	Serving Temperature

Notes

Ratings ☆ ☆ ☆ ☆ ☆

Beer Name

Brewery _____   Style _____

ABV _____   IBU _____   OG _____

Appearance		☆ ☆ ☆ ☆ ☆
Aroma		☆ ☆ ☆ ☆ ☆
Body		☆ ☆ ☆ ☆ ☆
Taste		☆ ☆ ☆ ☆ ☆
Finish		☆ ☆ ☆ ☆ ☆

Pairs With	Serving Temperature

Notes

Ratings   ☆ ☆ ☆ ☆ ☆

Beer Name

Brewery _____ Style _____

ABV _____ IBU _____ OG _____

Appearance		☆ ☆ ☆ ☆ ☆
Aroma		☆ ☆ ☆ ☆ ☆
Body		☆ ☆ ☆ ☆ ☆
Taste		☆ ☆ ☆ ☆ ☆
Finish		☆ ☆ ☆ ☆ ☆

Pairs With	Serving Temperature

Notes

Ratings ☆ ☆ ☆ ☆ ☆

Beer Name

Brewery _____ Style _____

ABV _____ IBU _____ OG _____

Appearance		☆ ☆ ☆ ☆ ☆
Aroma		☆ ☆ ☆ ☆ ☆
Body		☆ ☆ ☆ ☆ ☆
Taste		☆ ☆ ☆ ☆ ☆
Finish		☆ ☆ ☆ ☆ ☆

Pairs With	Serving Temperature

Notes

Ratings ☆ ☆ ☆ ☆ ☆

Beer Name

Brewery _____   Style _____

ABV _____   IBU _____   OG _____

Appearance		☆ ☆ ☆ ☆ ☆
Aroma		☆ ☆ ☆ ☆ ☆
Body		☆ ☆ ☆ ☆ ☆
Taste		☆ ☆ ☆ ☆ ☆
Finish		☆ ☆ ☆ ☆ ☆

Pairs With	Serving Temperature

Notes

Ratings ☆ ☆ ☆ ☆ ☆

Beer Name

Brewery _____ Style _____

ABV _____ IBU _____ OG _____

Appearance		☆ ☆ ☆ ☆ ☆
Aroma		☆ ☆ ☆ ☆ ☆
Body		☆ ☆ ☆ ☆ ☆
Taste		☆ ☆ ☆ ☆ ☆
Finish		☆ ☆ ☆ ☆ ☆

Pairs With	Serving Temperature

Notes

Ratings ☆ ☆ ☆ ☆ ☆

Beer Name _____

Brewery _____ Style _____

ABV _____ IBU _____ OG _____

Appearance		☆ ☆ ☆ ☆ ☆
Aroma		☆ ☆ ☆ ☆ ☆
Body		☆ ☆ ☆ ☆ ☆
Taste		☆ ☆ ☆ ☆ ☆
Finish		☆ ☆ ☆ ☆ ☆

Pairs With	Serving Temperature

Notes

Ratings ☆ ☆ ☆ ☆ ☆

Beer Name

Brewery _____   Style _____

ABV _____   IBU _____   OG _____

Appearance		☆ ☆ ☆ ☆ ☆
Aroma		☆ ☆ ☆ ☆ ☆
Body		☆ ☆ ☆ ☆ ☆
Taste		☆ ☆ ☆ ☆ ☆
Finish		☆ ☆ ☆ ☆ ☆

Pairs With	Serving Temperature

Notes

Ratings ☆ ☆ ☆ ☆ ☆

Beer Name

Brewery _____ Style _____

ABV _____ IBU _____ OG _____

Appearance		☆ ☆ ☆ ☆ ☆
Aroma		☆ ☆ ☆ ☆ ☆
Body		☆ ☆ ☆ ☆ ☆
Taste		☆ ☆ ☆ ☆ ☆
Finish		☆ ☆ ☆ ☆ ☆

Pairs With	Serving Temperature

Notes

Ratings ☆ ☆ ☆ ☆ ☆

Beer Name

Brewery _____ Style _____

ABV _____ IBU _____ OG _____

Appearance		☆ ☆ ☆ ☆ ☆
Aroma		☆ ☆ ☆ ☆ ☆
Body		☆ ☆ ☆ ☆ ☆
Taste		☆ ☆ ☆ ☆ ☆
Finish		☆ ☆ ☆ ☆ ☆

Pairs With	Serving Temperature

Notes

Ratings ☆ ☆ ☆ ☆ ☆

Beer Name	
Brewery	Style
ABV	IBU	OG

Appearance		☆ ☆ ☆ ☆ ☆
Aroma		☆ ☆ ☆ ☆ ☆
Body		☆ ☆ ☆ ☆ ☆
Taste		☆ ☆ ☆ ☆ ☆
Finish		☆ ☆ ☆ ☆ ☆

Pairs With	Serving Temperature

Notes

Ratings ☆ ☆ ☆ ☆ ☆

Beer Name

Brewery _____ Style _____

ABV _____ IBU _____ OG _____

Appearance		☆ ☆ ☆ ☆ ☆
Aroma		☆ ☆ ☆ ☆ ☆
Body		☆ ☆ ☆ ☆ ☆
Taste		☆ ☆ ☆ ☆ ☆
Finish		☆ ☆ ☆ ☆ ☆

Pairs With	Serving Temperature

Notes

Ratings ☆ ☆ ☆ ☆ ☆

Beer Name		
Brewery	Style	
ABV	IBU	OG

Appearance		☆ ☆ ☆ ☆ ☆
Aroma		☆ ☆ ☆ ☆ ☆
Body		☆ ☆ ☆ ☆ ☆
Taste		☆ ☆ ☆ ☆ ☆
Finish		☆ ☆ ☆ ☆ ☆

Pairs With	Serving Temperature

Notes

Ratings ☆ ☆ ☆ ☆ ☆

Beer Name

Brewery _____ Style _____

ABV _____ IBU _____ OG _____

Appearance		☆ ☆ ☆ ☆ ☆
Aroma		☆ ☆ ☆ ☆ ☆
Body		☆ ☆ ☆ ☆ ☆
Taste		☆ ☆ ☆ ☆ ☆
Finish		☆ ☆ ☆ ☆ ☆

Pairs With	Serving Temperature

Notes

Ratings ☆ ☆ ☆ ☆ ☆

Beer Name

Brewery _____ Style _____

ABV _____ IBU _____ OG _____

Appearance		☆ ☆ ☆ ☆ ☆
Aroma		☆ ☆ ☆ ☆ ☆
Body		☆ ☆ ☆ ☆ ☆
Taste		☆ ☆ ☆ ☆ ☆
Finish		☆ ☆ ☆ ☆ ☆

Pairs With	Serving Temperature

Notes

Ratings ☆ ☆ ☆ ☆ ☆

Beer Name

Brewery _____   Style _____

ABV _____   IBU _____   OG _____

Appearance		☆ ☆ ☆ ☆ ☆
Aroma		☆ ☆ ☆ ☆ ☆
Body		☆ ☆ ☆ ☆ ☆
Taste		☆ ☆ ☆ ☆ ☆
Finish		☆ ☆ ☆ ☆ ☆

Pairs With	Serving Temperature

Notes

Ratings ☆ ☆ ☆ ☆ ☆

Beer Name

Brewery _____   Style _____

ABV _____   IBU _____   OG _____

Appearance		☆ ☆ ☆ ☆ ☆
Aroma		☆ ☆ ☆ ☆ ☆
Body		☆ ☆ ☆ ☆ ☆
Taste		☆ ☆ ☆ ☆ ☆
Finish		☆ ☆ ☆ ☆ ☆

Pairs With	Serving Temperature

Notes

Ratings ☆ ☆ ☆ ☆ ☆

Beer Name

Brewery _____   Style _____

ABV _____   IBU _____   OG _____

Appearance		☆ ☆ ☆ ☆ ☆
Aroma		☆ ☆ ☆ ☆ ☆
Body		☆ ☆ ☆ ☆ ☆
Taste		☆ ☆ ☆ ☆ ☆
Finish		☆ ☆ ☆ ☆ ☆

Pairs With	Serving Temperature

Notes

Ratings ☆ ☆ ☆ ☆ ☆

Beer Name

Brewery _____ Style _____

ABV _____ IBU _____ OG _____

Appearance		☆ ☆ ☆ ☆ ☆
Aroma		☆ ☆ ☆ ☆ ☆
Body		☆ ☆ ☆ ☆ ☆
Taste		☆ ☆ ☆ ☆ ☆
Finish		☆ ☆ ☆ ☆ ☆

Pairs With	Serving Temperature

Notes

Ratings ☆ ☆ ☆ ☆ ☆

Made in the
USA
Columbia, SC